APPRA

AND APP

INTERVI

APPRAISAL
AND APPRAISAL
INTERVIEWING

by Ian Lawson

The Industrial Society

First published 1972 by
The Industrial Society
Robert Hyde House
48 Bryanston Square
London W1H 7LN
Telephone 071-262 2401

Second edition 1987
Revised 1988
Third edition 1989
Reprinted 1991, 1992
© *The Industrial Society, 1972, 1987, 1988, 1989*

ISBN 0 85290 412 6

British Library Cataloguing in Publication Data
Lawson, Ian
   Appraisal and appraisal interviewing — 3rd ed.
   1. Business firms. Personnel. Performance. Assessment.
   I. Title   II. Industrial Society   III. Series
   658.3'125

Typeset by Columns of Reading
Printed and bound in Great Britain by Belmont Press, Northampton

CONTENTS

FOREWORD

Whatever the discipline or level of management, the responsibilities of a manager are many and various. It is their job to produce results with essentially just two resources—people and time.

To maximise the potential of both, most managers need some reminders and basic guidelines to help them.

The Notes for Managers series provides succinct yet comprehensive coverage of key management issues and skills. The short time it takes to read each title will pay dividends in terms of utilising one of those key resources—people.

For people to give real commitment to their work they need to understand clearly what is expected of them—and why—and how they are progressing in terms of these objectives.

This short booklet reveals some of the most important points of good practice which have been identified from the growing field of appraisal and appraisal interviewing. It includes advice on the best available systems on installing and running a scheme, and on measuring performance.

ALISTAIR GRAHAM
Director, The Industrial Society

I

WHAT IS APPRAISAL?

1

THE IMPORTANCE OF
APPRAISAL TODAY

Staff appraisal is gaining increasing importance as a contributor to the success of organisations in industry, commerce and the public sector in Britain. Increased competition, rapid changes, reduced resources and employee expectations, have all combined in such a way that organisations are being expected to achieve more with less. Appraisal offers a method of developing the most important and valuable resource—people.

Consequently, many organisations are revising their existing appraisal schemes and introducing appraisal for all employees, not just 'staff' grades. In addition, the education sector, health and local authorities and many other employers are recognising the importance of appraisal. The method of appraising is also now tending towards openness, dialogue, and performance, rather than personality. Planned future actions are taking on more importance in comparison to past actions.

2

KEY ELEMENTS AND BASIC REQUIREMENTS OF APPRAISAL

Appraisal is one of the mechanisms to help gain people's commitment towards achieving the stated aims of the organisation. Therefore *the objective of appraisal is to help improve individual performance, realise potential and achieve better results for the organisation.*

Key elements

Any appraisal scheme should be concerned with these three essential areas:

- a review of past performance, from which lessons can be learned
- an identification of the future needs of the individual, the department and the organisation
- an action plan specifying what has to be done, by whom and by when.

Different organisations may have different objectives for their schemes and will need to identify these objectives— e.g. development, control, training, financial reward. What is called the appraisal scheme can be a reflection of these objectives. For example:

- staff assessment or annual report implies a situation in which job holders are told about their past performance

by their boss
- staff development or performance coaching suggests that the future should be considered and that this is done by discussion

The title and objectives should be compatible with the culture and aims of the organisation.

Basic requirements

Experience suggests that in the most successful systems:

- top management is committed and involved
- appraisals are carried out by the immediate boss
- all line managers receive training and the drill is monitored through the line
- in large organisations a senior person is accountable for monitoring the mechanics, consistency, and results of the scheme
- the method of looking at performance is objective and regular
- the job holders' views are taken into account
- the appraisal looks to the future as well as reviewing the past
- the objectives and workings of the scheme are explained to the appraisees.

3

BENEFITS TO BE GAINED
FROM AN APPRAISAL
SYSTEM

There are three main areas where benefits may be drawn from a successful scheme.

Benefits to the job holder

An appraisal system includes a drill which gives the job holder the opportunity to discuss all aspects of the job, with the boss, in-depth and away from the pressures of the daily work-load. It clarifies for the job holders how they can contribute best to the objectives of the department and the aims of the organisation. This forum helps identify strengths and weaknesses, building on the former and addressing the latter. It also gives clear direction on what is expected in the job, and involves the individuals in planning their work and their future. The input of other people and the support of their boss will also be discussed at this meeting. Finally, the recording of the interview and action plan means that a commitment has been made to make these things happen. It also means an individual should not have to start all over again if a new boss arrives.

Benefits to the boss

An important benefit of an appraisal system is that it creates the opportunity for managers to think seriously about what they expect of their people and, in particular, what their plans are for the period ahead. It provides a forum for recognition of new ideas and helps to tackle problem areas. It also clarifies and improves the relationship between the two parties and strengthens the position of the manager as leader. Appraisal is as much about developing managers as about developing staff.

Benefits to the organisation

Appraisal is a visible commitment by an organisation to recognising the importance of its people and this can be reflected in the morale of staff and be transmitted to potential employees. An organisation should aim for greater individual effectiveness and commitment in areas such as: corporate aims; succession planning; identification of training needs; feedback from employees; recurring problems; obtaining objective information (on performance) for use in business planning, promotion or salary decisions.

CHECKLIST

- Clarification of jobs and expectations.
- Shift from reacting to events, to controlling.
- Greater involvement and commitment from staff.
- An objective record of achievement and future action plans.
- Better use of human resources, training and succession planning.
- Improved results.

4

METHODS OF ASSESSING PERFORMANCE

Grading

Many systems rely to some extent on trait grading, that is, ticking a series of boxes which give grades for a number of qualities, for example:

Qualities	Unacceptable	*Below* average	Average	*Above* average	Excellent
Honesty					
Communication					
Initiative					
Co-operation					
Integrity					

The problem with this approach is that it concentrates on looking 'backwards', forces the job holder to react, is very subjective in interpretation, and tends towards middling. If there is a direct link to salary, it is likely that managers will be over-generous in their assessment: the so-called 'halo' effect. As it is straightforward it creates the opportunity for lazy managers to give insufficient thought to the process. Often gradings reflect boss–job holder relationships rather than achievement.

Organisations defend it on the grounds that: it forces a decision to be made about performance; it provides a guideline for salary reviews; it makes a statement about the manager. If it is to be used, ratings should be substantiated by written comments, guidelines on rating definition should be fully explained, and it should relate to performance not personality. Managers should be prepared to take into account job holders' comments and alter ratings if these are justified. Finally, it should be only part of a larger process which allows for development action to be discussed.

Written assessment

Written assessment requires consideration before committing pen to paper. The narrative of the appraiser needs to be specific and substantiative. However, it depends upon the questions asked or the discretion of the manager as to exactly what is recorded. The narrative often states more about the writing skills of the manager and the relationship between the manager and the job holder than it does about actual performance.

It will be more effective if it results from a discussion and if the job holder has given some thought to key questions before the interview, rather than the job holder simply reacting to the boss.

Management by Objective

In order to overcome the problems associated with personal qualities and subjective judgements, an objective method of appraising is required. The technique of management by objective (MBO) or an interpretation of it, when based upon measurable or recognisable job results, does provide a concrete way of assessing performance. It may be developed by ranking results against standards of performance to take into account the importance or difficulty of the tasks concerned.

The danger of MBO in practice is that some systems have become complicated. They can restrict discussion to a few objectives and miss other important areas. Rapid changes may not be reacted to or anticipated quickly enough.

Target setting

Increasingly, organisations are using target setting as the best means of measuring the performance of individuals. Such a system relies upon two key elements.

- Identifying key result areas for the job and setting standards of performance which are measurable, recognisable and achievable. These are ongoing and relate to the job.
- Setting targets which are priorities over and above the routine work. They are about change and development and relate to the individual job holder.

Target setting provides objectivity but is also dynamic, as it relies on a series of regular discussions between the two parties throughout the year, i.e. every one or two months, or quarterly. Records of targets, and success or failure, are for use at the main appraisal interview. Consequently, the annual interview does not reflect merely the last couple of months' work. Shortfalls can be identified and rectified at an early stage rather than being placed on the record at the end of the year as a failure to meet a target.

Providing that this system includes regular meetings and consultation and is not an imposition, it is the best method of meeting the need to have an objective appraisal scheme which is based upon a dialogue.

Checklist

- Methods of appraising people should be based upon performance, not personal qualities.
- The standards of performance expected must be made clear to the job holder.
- Systems must encourage forward-looking dialogue as well as looking at previous work.
- The job holder should be able to consider and inject information into the review of performance.
- Systems must include regular reviews in order to update the information base and to maintain impetus.

5

INTRODUCING AN
APPRAISAL SCHEME

Involvement of managers

If an appraisal scheme is to be successful it is important that line managers can identify with the scheme and that they perceive it as a useful tool. Therefore, it is essential to involve them in the evolution of such a scheme in order to increase their commitment. This can involve consultation during the early stages or trying out a draft scheme with representative departments and including their ideas for improving the scheme. This will help to sell the idea to the rest of the organisation.

Deciding on the scheme

There are a great many areas which need to be looked at when considering how a scheme will operate. The key steps to take before and during introduction are as follows.

1 Decide why a scheme is needed, what its objectives are and how it will help achieve the aims of the organisation.
2 Decide on the structure of the scheme—
   * paperwork
   * frequency and timing
   * who is involved
   * what support information will be produced
   * how information will be used (e.g. salary, training, career progress, etc.)
   * how it will be monitored.

3 Ensure that there is commitment at the most senior level.
4 Produce the required documentation.
5 Train the appraisers.
6 Communicate the objective and method of the scheme to all concerned.
7 Monitor the early stages closely and review its success at a pre-determined date.

Other factors to consider

Title

The name of the scheme can be important in introducing its purpose and in the effect it has on people's expectations. For example, 'annual report' suggests a purely backward-looking assessment with no dialogue. 'Performance coaching' suggests support and a forward-looking attitude, and emphasises performance, not personality.

Objectives

The organisation must make clear why it has installed or is installing a scheme. It is important to be realistic about results. Appraisal is normally about fine-tuning individual performance in the present job. Naturally, other objectives like planning, succession planning, and salary review can be introduced. It is vital that people see it as positive and not directly concerned with discipline, grievance or redundancy.

Mechanics

Is the scheme to be seasonal or rolling? This may depend on the link with money or corporate objective setting. Rolling schemes are easier for busy managers in theory; in practice an extended season, for example two months, gives a clear and realistic time span for managers to complete appraisals.

1 Appraisals should be conducted at least annually, but this must be supplemented by more frequent and regular reviews throughout the year.

2 The immediate boss should do the appraising as he/she is closest to the job holder's work. No-one should have to appraise more than 15 people. Using higher levels or personnel people weakens the boss–job holder relationship. The boss's boss (grandparent) should be involved to monitor action, check consistency of comments and gain upward information. Grandparents should be the first line of appeal—this is important to ensure fairness and gain credibility. Project management produces problems which can be mitigated by appointing a 'mentor' boss responsible for the individual's development. They will closely consult with others during the year. As appraisal is principally about looking forward, it should be the current boss who undertakes it even if new to the position. Clearly they will need to consult closely with others.

3 Personnel departments should prompt the system and can have a useful administration and collating role. They can also assess corporate and individual training requirements and succession planning.

4 Participants should be able to see what is being recorded and have an input into this. Action plans should be a working document.

5 Everyone should be appraised, and this should be done regularly throughout the year by means of review meetings. This will make the system dynamic and a part of the normal management function, and reduces the chance of surprises at the annual interview. The forms used may be different for managers, blue collar workers, and administration staff. In the case of junior staff, large developmental targets may not be as appropriate as they are to management or professionally qualified people.

6 Plans must be made for training all participants, supplying back-up paperwork, inducting new staff and training newly promoted managers. Decisions need to be made

on how the success of the scheme will be monitored and reviewed and the resulting involvement of line and personal staff.

Checklist

- Decide on the consultative process.
- Set dates for key stages of implementation.
- Design the mechanics of the scheme.
- Ensure commitment of top personnel.
- Produce support literature and paperwork.
- Train the appraisers.
- Communicate the objectives and methodology to all those concerned.
- Review the practical results of the scheme.

6

LINKING SALARY AND
PERFORMANCE

Some organisations do link salary increases to individual performance in order to encourage and develop, and to reflect the job holder's contribution to results.

Clearly, by this system there will then be a link between salary review and performance review. If people see this as an automatic link or if salary is discussed at the appraisal interview, then this can direct attention away from the main purpose of the system and reduce the honesty of the two parties. Managers may raise their judgements in order to avoid conflict; job holders may try to bargain down their targets in order to inflate achievement next time around.

Salary is a recognition of past performance. Appraisal is principally a discussion about future performance. Therefore, it is wise to have a different drill for each with two interviews being separated by time.

If recommendation on salary follows the interview, it is good practice to base this on performance and achievement against clearly understood objectives and to allow the job holder an input in the discussion of these results. However, other factors may affect any discretionary part of salary awards, e.g. length of service, position in scale, corporate or departmental results, and the amount of money available.

Checklist

- Have a separate drill for salary review and performance review.
- Relate salary only to those parts of performance which

can be substantiated.

- Ensure staff and managers are clear about factors which affect salary.

7

PAPERWORK

Appraisal depends upon dialogue and action, not paperwork. However, the paperwork is important because it imposes a drill to ensure that the meeting occurs and that a record is kept of what happens. It is also useful in that it ensures certain aspects of a person's performance are addressed and provides helpful feedback, and a means for senior managers to monitor the effectiveness of junior line managers and their appraisals.

With proper training and management experience, a blank sheet of paper may be more useful than an over-sophisticated system which takes little account of the pressures on busy line managers. Any form should include: a review of past performance against key result areas and specific targets; overall comments by the job holder, the boss and the boss's boss; a clear plan for development and action.

Support guidance notes to both appraiser and job holder should address the objectives of the scheme, the mechanics and structure of appraising, guidance on areas of performance to consider, and how to make the best use of the interview.

Paperwork should be as simple as possible. It will be more likely to succeed if it is geared towards line managers rather than management development specialists (*see* Appendix 1).

Checklist

- The paperwork is a vehicle, not an end in itself.
- It should be kept simple.

- Apart from forms, it should include guidance notes for appraisers and appraisees. (*See* Parts II and III for examples).

8

MEASUREMENTS OF PERFORMANCE

Standards of performance

A standard of performance relating to the job is a continuing yardstick for judging whether performance is at an acceptable level. It should be realistic, measurable or recognisable. Standards will relate to key result areas as in the job summary, e.g. sales, stock control, internal/external communication, supervision and administration.

Some jobs lend themselves very well to measurable standards, (e.g. sales people) while others may involve recognised methods of good practice. The six ways of considering how to answer the question 'What are the standards of performance that are expected of me?' are as follows.

- Numeric
  sales figures
  production levels
  defect levels
  paper flow.

- Deadlines
  projects
  turnaround of paper
  statutory
  regular meeting dates
  answering phone.

- Financial
  working within budget on sales and expenditure
  profit figures.

- Procedural stages of writing a computer programme
  internal liaison systems
  timings on replying to customer com-plaints
  giving information.

- Negative number of complaints
  feedback from colleagues.

- Recognisable approach to customers
  presentation at meetings
  typing errors and house style
  dress.

Target setting

Targets are priorities over and above the normal work. They are about change and development and relate to the individual.
Targets are set for the following reasons:

- to achieve results
- to get people to give their best performance
- to develop peoples' skills, abilities and knowledge
- to provide a challenge and a sense of achievement
- to improve communication between the boss and job holder.

Targets make an appraisal system dynamic and a part of the normal function of management. They should be set following consultation with the job holder as this will be more likely to gain commitment. Targets should be chal-lenging in order to motivate staff and should not be abandoned at the first sign of difficulty. It is important to be specific about the desired result and time-scale and not to set too many targets; say, no more than six at any time. By regularly reviewing progress and setting new targets, the system is able to become live rather than being an annual chore.

Examples of standards and targets

Key result area	Standard of performance	Target
Secretary Correspondence	Deal with correspondence within 48 hours	Reduce errors to not more than 2.5% by 31 December
Filing clerk Invoice files	Filing to be done on a daily basis	Clear backlog of unfiled invoices by next month's review
Salesperson Patch maintenance and development	Call rate to average 8/day at average 18 miles/call	To gain 3 new clients in October at min. £200 pcm
Scientist Research	To produce at least 3 research papers per year	Attend July conference on AIDS and present a 2000 word report at September meeting
Social worker Battered child cases	In category A cases visiting to be every two weeks followed by report to supervisor	Report on Social case 'X' at weekly intervals during May

Checklist

- Standards of performance need to be set against the important parts of the ongoing work.
- Targets are specific, one-off priorities and build on strengths, address weaknesses or explore new areas.
- Both should be set following consultation and reviewed regularly to assess progress.
- Records should be retained throughout the year by both parties.

9

ASSESSING POTENTIAL

There has recently been a general move away from judging career potential at the same interview as current performance is discussed. This has been because of the problems caused by managers not distinguishing between performance in present tasks and the potential different set of needs in a new job, often simply due to insufficient knowledge. Lack of opportunities, fear of the self-fulfilling prophecy of those not perceived to have potential, or disappointed expectations, are also factors. The spotting of potential also presupposes the identification of lack of potential and may restrict the beneficiaries to those who may fill a few high-level jobs to the detriment of developing potential on a broader range of skills.

If potential is to be discussed, it is important that promises are not made which cannot be kept. More often the discussion highlights areas to concentrate on and provides guidance to make people more 'marketable' should suitable vacancies arise. The best indicators are where people have shown consistent improvement in a job, particularly over a wide spread of disciplines and environments, or where they have coped with increased responsibilities. People's support for the work of colleagues or other departments and a non-parochial approach may also be usefully considered as indicators of potential.

Checklist

- Managers must check with senior management or personnel before making recommendations which may fall through.
- Promises should not be made unless they can be kept.

- Performance in similar job aspects or cultural environments may give an indication of potential.

10

APPRAISAL INTERVIEWING SKILLS

The linch pin for any system is the main appraisal interview which is normally done on an annual basis.

Preparation for the interview

Prior to the interview it is important to collate the information which should have been collected throughout the year, refer to previous records and speak with other people who are affected by the work of the job holder. Bosses should give plenty of thought to what they want to say, have ideas for the future, have done their homework regarding the possibility of secondments, training, etc., and try to anticipate the comments, problems, and aspirations which the appraisee may raise.

A brief meeting with the appraisee should be held to give notice of the interview, stress the objectives, outline areas for discussion and to hand over any relevant paperwork (see Appendix 1). Up to two hours should normally be allowed for an interview, although some interviews may not take this long. Back-to-back appointments should be avoided and managers should also avoid doing more than two per day. All ideas, key points and the structure of the interview should be recorded on paper to assist in conducting the interviews.

Conducting the interview

In order to promote discussion the room should be laid out informally, the appraisee welcomed and put at ease. It is imperative to start with a reminder of the purpose and structure of the interview. Although managers must give their view, it is useful to get the appraisee talking by using open questions, probing their answers, not interrupting and giving recognition where due. Problem areas must also be addressed, but as a sharing of a problem on performance, not a character assassination. There should be no surprises at the interview and managers must always be able to justify any comments they make. The use of summaries is to be recommended: to note key points, check acceptance, and move on to new areas. Even if it has not been a good year, an interview should always finish positively with a plan of action.

Follow-up

It is wise to write up interview notes immediately after the meeting and pass these on for further comments if required. Always set deadlines for this process so that completed forms are placed with the parties concerned as quickly as possible. Targets may have been set for the appraiser as well as the job holder (for example, to check availability of particular courses). Always ensure these are met in order to maintain the credibility of the system. Managers should then review progress with their people regularly throughout the year.

Checklist

- Allow time to prepare and give notification to the appraisee.
- Consider the previous period and prepare an overview.

- Consider departmental and individual needs for the future.
- Establish the purpose of the interview.
- Establish a dialogue and obtain the job holder's views.
- Use summaries throughout.
- Always finish on a positive note.
- Set deadlines to complete the process.
- Meet regularly to review progress throughout the year.

11

IMPLEMENTATION AND
MAINTENANCE

Having decided upon the scheme and its mechanics, a suitable timetable for implementation would include training all appraisers in:

- the objectives and benefits of the scheme, mechanics and paperwork
- setting standards and targets
- conducting an interview
- formulating an action plan
- ensuring it becomes part of the management function by holding regular reviews.

This is not the time to make changes in the paperwork otherwise the whole system may lose credibility.

Appraisees should also receive a face-to-face appreciation session on why and how the system is to run and what they can do to ensure they find it successful. Support literature should be supplied at these sessions.

After completing an initial round of appraisals it is a good idea to review the initial response and effectiveness and make improvements as necessary.

Maintenance

A great danger point for a successfully launched scheme is at two to three years, when people may become stale or run out of things to address. It is desirable to have refresher sessions and ensure newly appointed managers receive proper induction into their responsibilities as appraisers.

Senior management, in conjunction with personnel, should review the success of the scheme periodically, consult with those affected and make the changes required, particularly during the early stages.

Checklist

- Train all appraisers.
- Hold appreciation sessions for all other affected people.
- Ensure support literature is available.
- Address appraisal at induction sessions for new managers and appraisees.
- Hold refresher sessions every two to three years.
- Review the scheme periodically and communicate any changes.

Summary

Key points to consider in order to install and maintain an effective appraisal scheme are:

- gain involvement and commitment from the top
- let the scheme be owned by line managers
- appraise people on identifiable performance
- concentrate on the future
- review performance regularly
- train all appraisers and appraisees
- ensure people are clear about the scheme's objectives.

II

EXAMPLES OF APPRAISAL
SCHEMES

CONCORD LIGHTING
LIMITED
PERFORMANCE APPRAISAL

Notes for Guidance of Appraisers

Please read these notes carefully,
well before the appraisal interview

Concord Lighting Limited

The following should be presented to the job holder in advance of the interview.

To help you to prepare for your discussion with your managers, you may find it helpful to think about the following points, many of which may be raised during the course of your discussion.

1 What particular successes have you had during the period under review?
2 What difficulties have you faced?
3 Are there any constraints or problems which adversely affect your performance? How could these be alleviated?
4 Do you feel your manager has in any way restricted your capacity to perform your job?
5 What do you consider are your major strengths?
6 Are you sure of your exact authority?
7 Are the boundaries of your job clear?
8 Do you receive enough information about your performance?

9 What are your career ambitions?
10 Are your abilities being fully utilised in your current job?
11 What specific help could be given to you by:
- training
- action by colleagues
- action by management?

Action before the discussion

1 Read the job description, any previously agreed objectives and all information you have on the appraisee's work during the review period.
2 Fix a mutually convenient time and place and ensure the discussion will take place in private. You should allow at least two hours, even if all this time is not used.
3 Have a short meeting with the appraisee, at least five working days before the discussion, to explain the purpose (that is to review the work together, agree objectives and to plan for improved performance).

It is important to stress that the appraisal discussion will not be concerned with disciplinary or grievance issues. At this preliminary meeting the appraisee should be given their form and notes for guidance and asked to prepare for the discussion. Make any information you have used in your own preparation available to the interviewee.

Action during the discussion

1 Restate the purpose, emphasising the two-way nature of the discussion and the need to look forward.
2 Structure the interview on the basis of the previously agreed objectives and/or the job description.
3 Always ask for the appraisee's view first.

Ask open questions (for example, 'How has X gone?' or 'How do you feel about Y?' or 'Tell me, why did it happen?') rather than questions which only require 'Yes' or 'No' answers.

4 Seek solutions: too much emphasis on past problems will not be constructive.
5 Summarise each section of the discussion, to check your own understanding and to identify the required action. Note your summaries. This allows you to avoid taking notes throughout the interview.
6 Remember to discuss successes as well as problems. Most staff will be doing most of their work satisfactorily and this should be reflected in the interview.
7 Give an overall summary of the interview, clarifying the action the appraisee, you or others will take. Be precise and give dates wherever possible. Thank the appraisee.

Action after the interview

1 Complete your report immediately.
2 Give the report to the appraisee for him or her to add their comments.
3 Give the report to your Manager/Director for his or her comments.
4 Ensure all three parties have copies of the final form.

Don't forget

1 The appraisal interview is not the right occasion to discuss salaries.
2 Do not spend too much time looking back, it is principally an opportunity to look forward.
3 If job descriptions are revised, Group Personnel must be given a copy.

Concord Lighting Limited
Performance and
Development Record

Performance and development record

Date of review: ....

Name: ....

Job title: ....

Age: ....

Date appointed: ....

Name of appraiser: ....

Department director: ....

To be completed by the Appraising Manager:

SECTION A

1 Attainment of responsibilities and key activities over the previous period.

Objectives	Comments on attainment	Rating

2 Overall appraisal

RATING SCALE

1 Results achieved far exceed basic requirements in nearly all areas.

2 Results achieved exceed basic requirements in many respects.

3 Results achieved meet basic requirements.

4 Results achieved do not meet basic requirements.

SECTION B

Objectives for next appraisal period

1 Consider what objectives you feel would be the most important to achieve during the next appraisal period (6–12 months).

Major job objectives	Standards of performance

2 What training and development would lead to an improvement of your current performance?

SECTION C

Job holder's comments

Signed .... Date ....

Manager's manager's comments

Appraising Manager .... Date ....

Manager's Manager .... Date ....

2

CORNHILL INSURANCE
MANAGING BY RESULTS

Target setter's checklist

1 PAVE THE WAY

1.1 Obtain stationery.

1.2 Identify those involved this year.

1.3 Inform those who will be involved this year, giving at least 14 days' notice:
- arrange meeting, time and place—book room
- give 'Guide to Staff' (and any other assistance to those staff new to the system)
- hand 'Form A' completed appropriately to those involved.

2 PLAN THE INTERVIEW

2.1 Gather all information necessary to the discussions:
- corporate plan—be mindful of other targets at the location including your own
- 'Form B' of last year, where appropriate
- gather information relative to last year's targets— check levels of performance against the targets
- consult other departments managers if necessary.

2.2 Clarify in your own mind what it is you wish to achieve:
- improve performance
- staff development

- customer awareness.

The attached Target Setting Worksheet, which must be seen as a flexible discussion aid, may be helpful at this stage.

2.3 Decide how you will open the interview.

2.4 Decide the sequence of your discussions—probably following the format of the forms.

2.5 Prepare key pertinent questions:
- anticipate problem areas and make sure you have the facts
- write clear notes as interview reminders.

2.6 Above all, do your 'homework'; half-an-hour extra preparation is worth more than an hour's vacillation at the interview.

3   AT THE INTERVIEW

3.1 Be punctual.

3.2 Attend to 'courtesies':
- prevent interruptions
- seating arrangements
- smoking
- refreshments
- allow for note-taking by both parties.

3.3 Be professional:
- put 'targetee' at ease
- remind him/her of the purpose of the meeting
- in discussion ask probing questions
- listen to the answers
- summarise to ensure understanding
- make notes of salient points.

3.4 Review past year performance, where appropriate:
- against targets on previous Form B
- investigate reasons for over/under achievement
- ask 'open' probing questions
- check training plans (Section 3 of Form B).

3.5 Set future targets:
- ask for targetee's views of KRAs (Key Result Areas)

and the targets within them which may influence your own thinking

- make the targets realistic, reasonable and personal to the targetee—do not just pass your own targets on down the line.
- be absolutely clear on:
  - i what has to be achieved
  - ii when it has to be achieved
- aim for agreement—at least get acceptance
- discuss action plans
- assess and agree training or additional experience needs.

3.6 At the end of the interview:

- explain that there will be a short meeting for the report to be read and signed
- if necessary, agree a further meeting to finalise action plans which may have been too detailed to include in the main MBR (Management By Result) discussion
- explain to targetee that targets will be monitored regularly and new targets set where appropriate.

4 AFTER THE INTERVIEW

4.1 Complete Forms B and C, if applicable, as soon as possible and certainly before commencing the next interview.

4.2 Invite targetee to read and sign Form B. Any disagreement should be noted in Section 4.

4.3 Give targetee a copy of Section 2–Future Targets–or complete Form B if requested and encourage to use in self monitoring.

4.4 Collect and distribute copies of Forms B and C
- to Executive Head via local management
- to targetee for reference
- retain one copy for subsequent action.

4.5 Set up monitoring plan.

5 MONITORING PLAN

5.1 Monitoring is fundamental to the success of MBR.

5.2 Plan monitoring intervals.

5.3 Conduct progress reviews at those intervals.

5.4 Provide help and guidance if deemed necessary at the periodic monitoring meeting.

5.5 Targets are priorities and sometimes unforseen events cause priorities to change. Amend targets where essential to do so.

5.6 Set new targets as earlier ones are achieved.

5.7 Provide feedback to targetee on progress. This can be a powerful motivator.

6 TRAINING AND FUTURE EXPERIENCE

6.1 Consider how to put into effect the actions agreed in Section 3 of Form B.

6.2 Arrange for any appropriate experience to be under-taken (the training manager will pick up any matters related to in-company training from Form B).

6.3 When underway, check on effectiveness of programme.

7 CONCLUSION

The company is strongly committed to MBR. With everyone's enthusiastic participation this investment will be translated into the real benefit of improved performance so vital for the future.

MBR Target Setting Worksheet

As an aid only—subject to influence during discussions

Key result area	Target What do you want achieved?	When by?	Measurement of achievement What are the criteria it will be judged by? Are they MEASURABLE/ RECOGNISABLE? How?

MBR Target Setting and Performance Review

Form A

Confidential to Job Holder   **Review Year . . . . . .**

Performance Review—Self Assessment

Name ....

Please note that your annual review has been arranged for (date) ....

at .... am/pm with .... in ....

The purpose of this more formal discussion with your Manager or Supervisor is to review your performance over the year against your agreed targets; to consider the setting of new targets; and to identify ways in which your performance can be improved.

Arising from the discussion, any training needs you may have should be identified.

In preparation, please carefully consider the headings mentioned which are basic to this discussion. The form is simply a guide to help you prepare for useful discussion during your interview. You should complete the form which can be used for reference during the discussion if you wish. This form is merely a guide to your own thinking. It does not have to be shown to anyone. After the discussion it is for you to keep or destroy if you wish.

The value of the interview to you will depend chiefly on what you contribute to it. You may discuss any matters which in your opinion affect performance and productivity in your present job or may have a bearing on your future career.

1 List targets previously agreed	**2** What progress have you made towards meeting each of these targets?

3 What targets do you consider appropriate for the next year?

4 Are there any ways whereby your effectiveness in achieving your targets could be enhanced? Do you need more knowledge of particular matters?

5 Do you foresee any developments in your areas of accountability over the next year which could affect the achievement of future targets and therefore should be discussed?

6 Have you any other observations?

MBR Target Setting and Performance Review

Form B

Private and Confidential   **Review Year . . . . . .**

Performance Review Record Form

Name ....

Department branch ....

Job title ....

Job grade ....

Staff no. ....

Date of appointment to present position ....

Relevant qualifications (including degrees) ....

....

The purpose of this form is to review past performance, to set new targets and to improve the job holder's performance. Prior to the review you should study the individual's job description and previous review record forms so that your attention is focused on the targets that he/she has been trying to achieve.

1 Targets under review

List agreed targets	Target completion date	Comments on attainment against targets (Show degree of success including the extent of any over or under achievement)

Name .... Review Year ....

Performance Review Record Form

2 Future Targets
This section should be used to set targets for next year concentrating on Key Result Areas. Performance levels for each target should be defined in measurable terms.

List agreed targets	Target completion date	Levels of performance

Review Year ....

Performance Review Record Form

Name ....

Department branch ....

Job title ....

Job grade ....

Staff no. ....

Date of appointment to present position ....

Relevant qualifications (including degrees) ....

....

3(i) Action taken to improve performance
Reviewer should check that the measures contained in 3(ii) the previous year were actioned.

3(ii) Action needed to improve performance
Reviewer should consider what needs to be done to assist job holder in meeting new targets. What is required in the way of experience and training?

---

4 Any other relevant points and general comments

5 Prepared by ....

(Printed Name)

Signed ....

Job Title ....

Date ....

Signed by the job holder ....

Date ....

Seen by Executive Head ....

MBR Target Setting and Performance Review

Form C

Private and Confidential   **Review Year** . . . . . .

'Potential' List

Department branch ....

This return is confidential to Company Management. It is to be collated by the Branch Department Manager, after Performance Reviews have been completed, passed to the appropriate Executive Head and then to Personnel.

Its purpose is to identify those with ability to undertake immediately the next more senior job. Use the final column to denote which of these, if any, have the potential to undertake the next job but one.

Remember these forms will be prepared annually and someone who may not quite be ready to be included this year may qualify in future.

Name	Present job and grade (identify)	Next job and grade (identify)	Next but one job and grade (identify only if potential exists at present)

Signed .... (Branch/Departmental Manager)
Seen by Executive Head ....

3M

PERFORMANCE

APPRAISAL

Please write clearly.
Return to
The Personnel Department

(STRICTLY CONFIDENTIAL)

Name ....   Employee No. ....

Position ....   Age ....

Sales Force
or Dept ....   Joined 3M . . . . / . . . . / . . . .
                                                            D   M   Y

Region or
Location ....

Date of appraisal . . . . / . . . . / . . . .
                             D   M   Y

This appraisal covers performance during the previous _____
month period.

Length of time in position appraised:- _____ years.

> N.B. It is essential that the employee has been sent the
> Appraisal Preparation Form a week before the Appraisal
> is discussed with him or her.

Job performance

KEY RESPONSIBILITIES	RESULTS

(As defined in Job Description. Please use objective standards or measurements where possible and mention any external factors which may have influenced the results to be either over or under those expected.)

SPECIFIC IMPROVEMENT TARGETS	RESULTS

(Use objective standards or measurements where possible and mention any external factors which may have influenced the results to be either over or under those expected.)

N.B. A Target-setting form is enclosed for use by the Appraiser when setting targets *for the next performance review periods*.

Personal assessment

Please indicate any **major** strengths or weaknesses in the way in which the appraisee does the job which have significantly influenced the results achieved over the period under review. (For example, planning, organising, leading, controlling, decision making, communicating, creativity).

N.B. You may find the personal assessment checklist (in Appendix IV of the Performance Appraisal book) useful when completing this section.

Training and development

Please list below the **priority** training needs of this employee, if any, i.e. state the **specific improvements** required in terms of knowledge, skill, experience or attitudes. Where such steps are completely controllable by yourself, please place a target date by which time the action should be achieved. (Consideration should also be given to the employee's job description, and, if it no longer shows a true picture of the job, it should be revised.)

PRIORITY TRAINING NEEDS

– 5 –

WHAT ACTION WILL YOU BE TAKING TO DEVELOP THIS EMPLOYEE?	TARGET DATE

WHAT ACTION WILL BE TAKEN BY THE EMPLOYEE TO DEVELOP HIMSELF/HERSELF?	

WHAT ACTION DO YOU RECOMMEND SHOULD BE TAKEN BY THE PERSONNEL DEPARTMENT

(N.B. Prior discussion with the Personnel Department is often advisable before recommendations are made).

Noted by Personnel Department ....

Comments

1 Comments of the Appraiser (include comments on the Appraisal Preparation Form, if completed, and on any other relevant matter not already covered on pages 1–5).

2 Expressed interests in other positions or type of work.

3 Comments of the Reviewer.

Overall performance rating

Using the descriptions below as a guide, place a cross in the box in which the overall performance is best represented. Consider all aspects of performance carefully, particularly major key responsibilites, giving most weight to those which are most important in this position.

1	2	3	4	5
Inadequate below job requirements and not improving	Progressing below job requirements but improving	Good: met major job requirements	Very good performance in all major areas of responsibility	Excellent performance in every aspect of the job, both major and minor

PREVIOUS APPRAISAL

Date . . . . / . . . . / . . . .   (Omit if this does not refer to the
    D   M   Y   present job).

1	2	3	4	5

Final comments of the Employee (optional)

Appraised by:
(Position) ....   (Signed) ....

Reviewed by:
(Position) ....   (Signed) ....

Acknowledged by employee (Signed) ....

Date . . . . / . . . . / . . . .
    D   M   Y

III

APPENDICES

APPENDIX 1

PERFORMANCE APPRAISAL

A minimum organisation policy.

1 All employees shall have a discussion at least once a year with their manager about their performance. The discussion should recognise good performance and address weaker areas. Most of the content should relate to the future and should result in a specific plan for targets, training and development to help the individual improve.

2 The immediate line manager is responsible for seeing that this is done.

3 The discussion shall take place AT LEAST once a year.

4 Both parties should prepare for the interview and have an input on previous performance and priorities for the future.

5 The conclusions of the manager AFTER the interview shall be written on the appropriate form and individuals shall have the opportunity to add written comments if they wish.

6 Either during the interview, or soon after, a limited number of important targets shall be set on areas of work where progress is needed during the coming period. The person accountable, the timescale and result required should be clearly indicated.

7 Performance against these targets and key result areas should be reviewed regularly throughout the year.

APPENDIX 2

APPRAISAL—JOB HOLDER'S CHECKLIST

Job holder's checklist for use in preparation for appraisal and target setting interviews.
Difficulties which hinder effective performance.

1 Are you sure of the exact boundaries of your job?
   • Is there any overlap—two people each believing they are responsible for a certain area of work?
   • Is there any uncertainty—areas where you are not absolutely sure whether this item is your responsibility at all?
   • Are there areas not covered—areas for which no one seems to take any responsibility?
2 Are you sure of your exact authority?
   • What are the limits of authority in each area of work?
   • Are these limits high enough/too high?
   • In what areas are decisions left to your discretion?
   • In what areas do you need more room to use your discretion?
   • In what areas would you like more room to use your discretion?
3 What level of performance have you reached in each of the areas of your accountability and against your targets?
   What restricting factors prevent effective job performance?
   • Money—is the departmental budget reasonable/too high/too low?
   • Admin. resources—is the equipment satisfactory for the job? is the recruitment geared to your needs?
   • Communication—do you have adequate warning of changes? Sufficient information on matters affecting the work? Communication of management thinking?
   • Knowledge—what other knowledge would help you in your work?
   • Other departments—is there sufficient liaison with other departments i.e. those from whom you receive work and those to whom you pass work?
   • Other difficulties—any other difficulties which hamper you: lack of space, poor floor planning, awkward access, lack of prompt attention to maintenance of machines, etc?

4 Do you have adequate information on your progress towards targets?

5 What specific assistance can be given to help you?
Invitation to say constructively what:
- you personally need (perhaps training)
- what colleagues can do to help
- what management can do to help.